# Pearls
*from*
# Proverbs

## VALERIE WILSON

REGULAR BAPTIST PRESS
1300 North Meacham Road
Schaumburg, Illinois 60173-4806

PEARLS FROM PROVERBS

© 2000

Regular Baptist Press • Schaumburg, Illinois

1-800-727-4440 • www.regularbaptistpress.org

All rights reserved

Printed in U.S.A.

RBP5246 • ISBN: 0-87227-208-7

Third printing—2003

# Contents

# Dedicated

*to the women who have attended the Winning Weighs program
at First Baptist Church, Arlington Heights, Illinois,
and who have encouraged me by their response to the
study of God's Word.*

# Preface

The book of Proverbs is like a lovely string of pearls. One proverb after another is strung together to make the whole. The purpose of this study is to look at ten of those pearls—ten themes that are developed in Proverbs.

Because of the nature of Proverbs, it is difficult to do a verse-by-verse study. Instead, it is better to find what the book says on a given subject and study that topic. This study is arranged in that way.

In addition to discovering what Proverbs says on a given topic, you will look at other supporting passages throughout Scripture, and you will consider Biblical people who exemplify each truth. Each lesson closes with an opportunity for you to put the truths of Proverbs into practice in your own life, as well as a suggestion for praying the truths of Proverbs to the Lord.

I would encourage you to read one chapter of Proverbs each day during the weeks and months of this study. (You can coordinate your reading with the calendar; e.g., read chapter 1 on the first day of the month, chapter 2 on the second day.) In each day's reading, note a specific verse to meditate on during the day. Repeated exposure to the great themes in Proverbs will help you realize—and practice—the truths of this book.

It is my prayer that this study of Proverbs will enrich your spiritual life; that it will be practical for everyday life; and that these pearls will become part of your "wardrobe" in the days ahead.

# The Pearl of Wisdom

*"How much better is it to get wisdom than gold! and to get understanding rather to be chosen than silver!" (Proverbs 16:16).*

If you were told you could have any one thing your heart desired, what would you request? Would it be a specific sum of money? relief from physical pain? a mate (or a different mate)? a new home? a different job? a slimmer body size? The way each of us would answer that question reveals something about us, doesn't it?

A man in Bible times was presented with this exact opportunity. He could ask for anything he wanted. His answer—and a major theme in the book of Proverbs, which he wrote—is astonishing. We will look at him and the request he was granted as we start this study of Proverbs.

People with very little Bible knowledge know something about the book of Proverbs. We often think of a proverb as a wise saying, and it is that. The word is from a verb that means "to be like, to be compared with." "A proverb, then, is a statement that makes a comparison or summarizes a common experience."[1] The book contains maxims, poetry, short parables, and pithy questions—all designed to help the reader know how to live wisely and godly in an ungodly world.

The principal writer of the book was Solomon (Proverbs 1:1), although chapter 30 was written by a man named Agur and chapter 31 by King Lemuel. We know little about these men, but we know a great deal about Solomon.

## The Writer

1. Read 2 Samuel 12:24. Who were Solomon's parents? *David Bathsheba*

2. Look in the marginal references in your Bible or in a Bible dictionary. What does the name "Solomon" mean? *Peace*

3. (a) What other name did Solomon have (2 Samuel 12:25)? *Jedidiah*

   (b) What did it mean? *loved by the Lord*

David was the second king of the nation of Israel. Before his death, he proclaimed that Solomon would succeed him on the throne (1 Kings 1:28-40).

4. Read 1 Kings 2:2 and 3. (a) What was David's final charge to his son? *be strong walk in the ways of the Lord*

   (b) What would be the result if Solomon did this? *he may prosper his line will always have a king in Israel*

Soon after David's death, God appeared to Solomon in a dream and told Solomon to ask of Him anything he wanted.

5. Read 1 Kings 3:5-9. What was Solomon's request? *a discerning heart*

6. Read 1 Kings 3:10-14. What was God's answer?

*a wise + discerning heart*
*riches*
*honor*

7. Solomon's wisdom was put to the test right away. Summarize the event that is recorded in 1 Kings 3:16-28.

*2 prostitutes - 1 kid*

In New Testament times Jesus identified Solomon as a wise man (Matthew 12:42), and even today we use the expression "the wisdom of Solomon." Unfortunately, Solomon did not always live wisely. He allowed his wealth and his many wives to turn his heart from the Lord (1 Kings 11:1-6). However, God used Solomon during his lifetime as a writer of inspired Scripture: the majority of the book of Proverbs, which extols wisdom; Song of Solomon, a beautiful love story; Ecclesiastes, which describes the emptiness and folly of a life lived apart from God.

## Understanding Wisdom

8. Using a standard dictionary, define knowledge and wisdom; distinguish the differences between them.

• Knowledge

• Wisdom

• Differences

9. Are all "smart" people wise? Can an uneducated person be wise? Explain your answers.

> In the spiritual realm a person who possesses *hokmah* [the Hebrew word for "wisdom" used 45 times in Proverbs] in reference to God is one who is both knowledgeable and experienced in following God's way. So in the Bible's Wisdom literature being wise means being skilled in godly living. Having God's wisdom means having the ability to cope with life in a God-honoring way.[2]

10. Read Proverbs 2:6. Who is the source of wisdom?   *God*

11. Read Proverbs 9:10. (a) What is the beginning of wisdom?   *Lord*

*fear of the*

(b) What do you think this phrase means? Use your dictionary.

(c) How does fearing God help us have wisdom? (Refer to the definition of wisdom.)

## The Value of Wisdom

12. Read Proverbs 3:13-18. In this passage wisdom is personified as a woman; the pronouns "her" and "she" refer to wisdom. According to these verses, what are the values of wisdom?

*profitable*
*better returns than gold*
*precious          blessings*
*long life*
*peace*

13. What does Proverbs 16:16 teach about the value of wisdom?

*it is better than riches*

14. Why do you think Solomon placed such high value on wisdom?

*wisdom — what is important,*
*what to worry about,*
*ability to live for God*

## The Wise Person

15. The following verses tell us about the wise person and how she lives. Read each verse and note the characteristic of the wise person.

- Proverbs 3:13  *Blessed*

- Proverbs 9:8, 9; 17:10  *loving, able to learn,*

- Proverbs 12:15  *listens to advice*

• Proverbs 14:16 *fears the Lord, shuns evil*

• Proverbs 16:21 *discerning*

• Proverbs 3:35 *honorable*

## Christ, the Wisdom of God

16. Read 1 Corinthians 1:24. (a) How is Jesus Christ described in this verse? *the power + wisdom of God*

(b) Read verse 30. What did Christ become for us?
*wisdom of God*

Man apart from God knows only worldly wisdom. (See 1 Corinthians 3:19 and 20 and James 3:15-17.) Worldly wisdom may help a person survive in this world, but it does nothing to help a person prepare for eternity. The wisdom of which Solomon wrote—the skill to live a godly life—comes only from being rightly related to Jesus Christ.

Sin broke our relationship with God. We have all sinned (Romans 3:23). Jesus died on the cross in our place, taking on Himself the punishment for our sin (Romans 5:8; 1 Peter 2:24). When we place our trust in the work He did and receive the free gift of salvation (John 1:12; Ephesians 2:8, 9), the relationship is restored.

The plan of salvation is so simple—and so opposite of what man strives to do; namely, work to win God's favor—that Paul said "the preaching [message] of the cross is . . . foolishness" to people who do not receive God's gift (1 Corinthians 1:18). But "it pleased God by the foolishness of preaching to save them that believe" (1 Corinthians 1:21). To those who believe, Christ is our wisdom and righteousness and sanctification and redemption. In Christ alone can a person be truly wise.

Jesus Christ is made to me, All I need, all I need,
He alone is all my plea, He is all I need.
Wisdom, righteousness and power, Holiness this very
　　hour;
My redemption full and free, He is all I need.

*—Unknown*

## Proverbs in Practice

1. Explain the wisdom described in Proverbs in your own words.

2. How can a person who is uneducated as far as this world is concerned be wise in God's sight?

3. Why do you think the wisest man who ever lived (apart from Jesus Christ) lived foolishly at the end of his life?

4. Have you believed the "foolish" message of the preaching of the cross? Has Jesus Christ been made wisdom to you?

5. For what life situations do you need wisdom this week? Claim the promise of James 1:5 for those situations.

## Proverbs in Prayer

*Dear Heavenly Father, at the start of this study in Proverbs, I come to You, asking for wisdom. You have said that it is better to get wisdom than to have gold. Lord, I want Your wisdom! I want to respond to life in a way that pleases You. Having Your wisdom will help me avoid evil and the things that displease You. I honor and revere You as the infinite God, Who is all wisdom. And I come to You in the name of the Lord Jesus, in Whom are hidden all the treasures of wisdom and knowledge. Amen.*

Notes

1. John F. Walvoord and Roy B. Zuck, *The Bible Knowledge Commentary: Old Testament* (Wheaton, Ill.: Victor Books, 1985), p. 903.

2. Walvoord and Zuck, p. 902.

# The Pearl of Awe and Reverential Trust

*"The fear of the LORD is the beginning of wisdom: and the knowledge of the holy is understanding" (Proverbs 9:10).*

**M**ost children—at least for a few years of their lives—are probably deterred from negative behavior because they have a certain respect for their parents. These children know that moms and dads have various punishments available to them to mete out, punishments that range from being unpleasant at best to downright painful at worst. If you were to ask these children, many of them would affirm that they love their parents. But at the same time they have a healthy respect for their parents' authority.

In the spiritual realm something similar should be true of God's children—only on a much greater scale. While we love Him and want to please Him because we love Him, we also need a healthy dose of what the Bible calls "the fear of the LORD." Jerry Bridges says, "The fear of God is the animating and invigorating principle of a godly life."[1] Let's see how Proverbs develops this theme.

## Understanding the Fear of the Lord

1. Look at question 11 in lesson 1 (p. 10). How did you define "fear of the Lord"?

The dictionary indicates that the English word "fear" can mean reverential awe of someone, as of God. The Hebrew word that is translated "fear" has the idea of reverence or worship. So the "fear of the Lord" does not refer to being afraid or to having a dread of something. Rather, it refers to an attitude we are to have toward God; namely, we are to recognize Who He is and respond to Him accordingly. The fear of the Lord is "reverential awe—a mixture of fear, veneration, wonder, and admiration, all directed toward God Himself."[2]

2. Look up each of the following verses and jot down what each one says about God.

   • Deuteronomy 33:27 *our refuge, protection against our enemy*

   • Malachi 3:6 *does not change*

   • 1 Kings 8:27 *the heavens can not contain Him he is so great*

   • Psalm 99:9 *Holy*

   • Psalm 11:7 *righteous*

   • Psalm 135:6 *does what he pleases*

   • Genesis 18:25 *judge*

   • Genesis 17:1 *God almighty*

   • Psalm 139:7-11 *Can see all*

• Acts 15:18 *has been knowledges*

• 1 John 4:7, 8 *love comes from God*

When our view of God is correct, we will respect Him and respond to Him in awe and reverential trust. We will "fear" Him.

> Immortal, invisible, God only wise,
> In light inaccessible hid from our eyes,
> Most blessed, most glorious, the Ancient of Days,
> Almighty, victorious—Thy great name we praise.
>
> To all, life Thou givest—to both great and small,
> In all life Thou livest—the true life of all;
> We blossom and flourish as leaves on the tree,
> And wither and perish—but naught changeth Thee.
>
> Great Father of glory, pure Father of light,
> Thine angels adore Thee, all veiling their sight;
> All praise we would render—O help us to see
> 'Tis only the splendor of light hideth Thee!
> —*Walter Chalmers Smith*

## The Benefits of Fearing the Lord

Most of the time when Solomon talked about the fear of the Lord in Proverbs, he did so in terms of the benefits of fearing the Lord.

3. Read Proverbs 14:26. (a) What is the benefit in this verse?

*a secure fortress + a refuge for his children*

(b) Look back at the characteristics of God (question 2). How can knowing God better help us have "strong confidence" in Him?

4. Read Proverbs 14:27. (a) What is the benefit in this verse?

*life*

(b) Relate this verse to both physical and spiritual life. How does the fear of the Lord relate to the idea of a fountain of life?

*God gives life eternal & fulfillment in this life*

5. Read Proverbs 15:16 and 19:23. (a) What are the benefits in these verses? *less trouble*

(b) Why would it be easier for a person to be content if she had a correct view of God?

6. Read Proverbs 1:7 and 9:10. (a) What is the benefit in these verses?

*begining of knowledge*

(b) How does Colossians 2:3 help you understand this concept?

*the treasure of knowledge is hidden in God*

7. Read Proverbs 28:14. What is the benefit in this verse?

*blessings*

8. Read Proverbs 16:6. What is the benefit in this verse?

*avoiding evil*

## The Results of Not Fearing the Lord

You have heard or read of individuals who deny either the existence of God or at least His involvement in the lives of His creatures. The Bible has a name for such people: "The fool hath said in his heart, There is no God" (Psalm 14:1). To deny the existence of God—or to live as though He did not exist—is to fit the Bible's definition of a fool. Such a person lives in direct contrast to the person who fears the Lord. Just as positive benefits come to the person who chooses to fear the Lord, so negative consequences await the one who chooses to turn from God. (Note Proverbs 1:29—"They . . . did not *choose* the fear of the LORD" [emphasis added].)

9. Read each of the following verses and note the negative result.

• Proverbs 28:14 *trouble*

• Proverbs 19:23 *trouble*

• Proverbs 10:27 *shortened life*

• Proverbs 1:29-32 *death, destruction,*

People who choose not to recognize God and respond to Him in awe and reverential trust will one day be filled with dread in His presence. "It is a fearful thing to fall into the hands of the living God" (Hebrews 10:31).

## The Positive Example of Joseph

10. Read Genesis 39:1-9. Joseph was a young man who feared God. How do we know that from this passage?

*because God's blessings were on him + on his household he would not sin against God*

11. Read Genesis 50:15-22. How does this passage demonstrate Joseph's recognition of God and right response to Him?

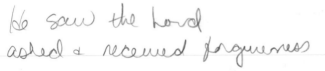

*he could have held a grudge against his brothers for what they did to him instead he forgave them + promised to provide for them*

## The Positive Example of Isaiah

12. Read Isaiah 6:1-8. (a) What kind of experience did Isaiah have?

*He saw the Lord asked + received forgiveness*

(b) How did he respond to this experience?

*Volunteered to go for the Lord*

## The Negative Example of Pharaoh

13. Read Exodus 5:1 and 2. What was Pharaoh's reaction when Moses confronted him with the directive from the Lord God?

*I do not know the Lord & I will not follow his commands*

Pharaoh should have known better than to defy God in this way, but he refused to recognize Who God is. As Bridges notes, "Pharaoh was neither in awe of God, nor afraid of His judgments."[3] Pharaoh certainly experienced all the negative results of not fearing the Lord, culminating in the death of his firstborn (Exodus 12:29, 30).

## Our View of God

"If there is anything we need during life's baffling and bewildering experiences, it is not an explanation, but just a fresh, new look at God."[4] Perhaps the God you've been looking at is too small. Perhaps you have made God into a "kinder, gentler" Being, One with whom you can feel comfortable. If your description of God is "the man upstairs," you do not have a Biblical view of God; you do not fear Him.

Or perhaps God seems far away and too unapproachable. Perhaps "fear" to you is dread rather than awe. This is not a Biblical view of God either. He is not a tyrant in the heavens, waiting to mete out punishment.

Do you want to know what God is really like? Centuries ago some men said to the Lord Jesus, "Shew us the Father, and it sufficeth us" (John 14:8). Jesus' answer was simple and direct: "He that hath seen me hath seen the Father" (John 14:9). "No man hath seen God at any time; the only begotten Son, which is in the bosom of the Father, he hath declared him" (John 1:18). "God wrapped Himself in human flesh and placed Himself on display. . . . Jesus is the mirror of God—the precise image of His Person—the exact replica of His Being. . . . [God] bridged the distance completely in Christ and made Himself accessible to us all."[5]

The fear of the Lord—the recognition of Who God is and the right response to that knowledge—is the cornerstone of life. Can you describe yourself as a person who fears the Lord? "Favour is deceitful, and beauty is vain: but a woman that feareth the LORD, she shall be praised" (Proverbs 31:30).

## Proverbs in Practice

1. To enlarge your view of God, review the list of God's characteristics in question 2.

2. Read the book of Psalms over a period of time and make a list of all the things those songs say about God.

3. How do you think you can tell if a person fears the Lord or not?

4. What specific steps will you take to become a woman who is known as one who fears the Lord?

## Proverbs in Prayer

*Almighty God, as I come to You in prayer, I express my awe of You. I choose to fear and adore You. When I honor You for Who You truly are, I have confidence in You and all You want to do for me. I would rather grow in my knowledge of You than to acquire great treasure. I am satisfied. I realize that fearing You is a strong deterrent to evil in my life. Above all, fearing You leads to true happiness. God, help me to fear You more reverently, love You more deeply, and obey You more completely. I make these requests in the name of Your Son, Who has helped me understand Who You are. Amen.*

Notes

1. Jerry Bridges, *The Joy of Fearing God* (Colorado Springs: WaterBrook Press, 1997), p. 25.
2. Bridges, p. 19.
3. Bridges, p. 20.
4. Don Baker, *A Fresh New Look at God* (Portland, Ore.: Multnomah Press, 1986), p. 7.
5. Baker, p. 58.

# The Pearl of Humility

*"When pride cometh, then cometh shame: but with the
lowly is wisdom" (Proverbs 11:2).*

She was probably the most humble person I have ever known. She
was a simple woman with little of this world's goods; she was small
of stature; many people would have considered her unlearned. But she
was a giant to all who knew her, this humble servant woman. Because
my mother was an invalid—and because my father was a pastor and we
lived in a parsonage—this dear woman served our family in more ways
than I probably even know. And I'm sure I did not adequately appreciate
all she did for us. But the things I remember about her are striking. She
used a cotton swab and cleaned even the keyholes in our doors! She
made rolls that could easily have been served in the finest of banquet
halls. I have another memory of her: her Bible. One day I looked at it. I
was amazed! On every page I saw her handwritten pencil notes. Her love
for and study of God's Word were the bedrock on which her humble service was founded. She would be embarrassed to know I had used her as
an example of humility. Goldie, which is the only name we ever used for
her, is in Heaven now. She's probably looking for keyholes to clean!

Humility is one of the most difficult virtues to describe—and, for
many of us, one of the most illusive to attain. In most areas of life we can
determine if we are making progress. We can see evidences of greater
love, more patience, more self-control, increased joy, and so on. But as
soon as we decide we have more humility, we have lost it; or so it seems.
We chuckle to ourselves that the person who wrote the book *My Humil-*

*ity and How I Attained It* was, in reality, proud. But humility is a frequent theme in Scripture, especially in Proverbs. We need to understand it in order to add this pearl to the wardrobe of our lives.

## Humility toward God

"Humility toward God is akin to the fear of God: it begins with a high view of God's person. As we see God in his majesty, awesomeness, and holiness, we are humbled before him."[1] The Bible records the response of several individuals who were privileged to understand something of the greatness of God.

1. Read Exodus 3:1-6. What was Moses' response to God?

   *he hid his face*

2. Read Job 42:1-6. What was Job's response?

   *despise myself + repent*

3. A man named Agur wrote Proverbs 30. Read verses 2-4. How did he respond to what he knew about God?

   *felt he was ignorant*

4. Read Revelation 1:10-17. What was John's response?

   *fell to God's feet*

5. Read Revelation 4:9-11. What was the response of the twenty-four elders to the glorified Lamb of God?

   *lay down their crowns + worship God*

In each of these examples, the individuals responded to the greatness of God in humility. They saw themselves as they were in light of Who God is.

6. Read Proverbs 11:2. The word "lowly" is a synonym for "humble." What is the relationship between humility and wisdom? (Review the meaning of wisdom in lesson 1.) *humility brings wisdom*

## Humility with Regard to Self

One aspect of humility is to understand Who God is; another aspect is to understand who we are. "Humility with regard to ourselves . . . consists in ascribing all that we are, all that we have, and all that we have accomplished to the God who gives us grace."[2]

7. Humility with regard to self means recognizing that all we are and all that we have comes from God. Summarize the truth of each of the following verses.

- 1 Corinthians 4:7 *why are we different from anyone else — because of what God has given us*

- Isaiah 26:12 *all that we have accomplished God has done*

- 1 Corinthians 15:10 *By the grace of God, I am what I am*

• Deuteronomy 8:17, 18  *God gives us our abilities*

8. Read Proverbs 25:6 and 7 and Proverbs 27:2. What do these verses
teach us about regarding ourselves properly before other people?

*Don't exault ourselves before others,
let others praise us*

9. What are some ways a humble person can respond to sincere
compliments and praise?

*thank you*

10. Read Proverbs 16:18 and 18:12. Compare those verses with Luke
14:11 and James 4:10. What do these four verses teach us?

*Pride → destruction, fall
humility comes before honor
humble yourself God will lift you up*

## The Supreme Example

11. Read Philippians 2:3-11. (a) About Whom is this passage speaking?

*Jesus*

(b) How did He exemplify humility? (See also Matthew 20:26-28.)

*became man, Servant,
obediant to death*

(c) How do verses 9-11 illustrate the truth you discovered in
question 10?

*Jesus was exalted to highest place,
name above every name
every knee bow @ his name
every tongue confers He is Lord*

(d) What are we to do based on this example (verse 5)?

*Our attitude should be the
same as Jesus'*

O to be like Thee! blessed Redeemer,
This is my constant longing and prayer;
Gladly I'll forfeit all of earth's treasures,
Jesus Thy perfect likeness to wear.

O to be like Thee! lowly in spirit,
Holy and harmless, patient and brave;
Meekly enduring cruel reproaches,
Willing to suffer others to save.

O to be like Thee! O to be like Thee,
Blessed Redeemer, pure as Thou art!
Come in Thy sweetness, come in Thy fullness;
Stamp Thine own image deep on my heart.

*—Thomas O. Chisholm*

## The Antithesis of Humility

As hard as it may be to define and describe humility, we are quite ca-
pable of recognizing the opposite trait: pride.

12. Read Proverbs 21:4. What is God's evaluation of pride?
*the lamp of the wicked
sin*

13. Read Proverbs 16:5 and 6:16 and 17. What is God's attitude toward
pride? *detests the proud, they will be
punished*

14. According to Proverbs 11:2, what does pride eventually bring?

*disgrace*

15. Proverbs 16:18 is a familiar—though often misquoted—proverb. What does it teach about pride? *destruction is the result*

16. Read Daniel 4:28-37. (a) What was Nebuchadnezzar's attitude at the beginning of this passage?

*proud of what he had built*

(b) What happened to him?

*God sent him away from people + had him eat grass like animals*

(c) What was his attitude at the end of the passage?

*humble — praise + exault + glorify God*

17. Read Acts 12:20-23. (a) What was King Herod's attitude?

*the people called him a god + he did not deny it*

(b) What was the outcome for this proud king?

*death*

The pearl of humility is like a precious jewel; it beautifies the one who wears it. Before we can wear the jewel, however, we must recognize with the apostle Paul that "in me (that is, in my flesh,) dwelleth no good thing" (Romans 7:18). We must come humbly to the Savior, in childlike submission, and confess that all our righteousnesses are like filthy rags (Matthew 18:3, 4; Isaiah 64:6). We must realize that we cannot save ourselves, that our works are useless, and that only in Christ is salvation possible. Once we have trusted Jesus Christ as our personal Savior, we can obey the command to "put on . . . humbleness of mind" (Colossians 3:12).

## Proverbs in Practice

1. What is your personal response to the greatness and holiness of God?

2. Are there areas in your life where you tend to be proud? Recognize pride as the sin that it is and confess it to God (1 John 1:9).

3. Practice some responses you can use when people compliment you.

4. Look for opportunities to put other people ahead of yourself (Philippians 2:3, 4).

## Proverbs in Prayer

*Dear God, help me understand how to live humbly. My natural tendency is toward pride, and a proud heart is a sinful heart. When my heart is lifted up within me, remind me that pride leads to destruction. I want to have the mind of Christ, Who modeled humility when He left the glories of Heaven and came to this earth. I pray in His name, amen.*

Notes

1. Jerry Bridges, *The Practice of Godliness* (Colorado Springs: NavPress, 1983), p. 91.
2. Bridges, *The Practice of Godliness*, p. 97.

# The Pearl of Honesty and Integrity

*"The integrity of the upright shall guide them: but the perverseness of transgressors shall destroy them" (Proverbs 11:3).*

Whoever said "Honesty is the best policy" was speaking Biblical truth whether he knew it or not. Throughout the pages of the Bible, honesty and integrity are extolled; dishonesty, falseness, and duplicity are to be avoided. In the first century of American history, Biblical—or at least moral—values were esteemed. The anecdotal account of George Washington's honesty is summed up in the words, "I cannot tell a lie." The sixteenth president was known then and now as "Honest Abe," a nickname he earned because he was a man of integrity.

How different is the record of our country now. Biblical values not only are not esteemed, they are ridiculed. With presidential nicknames like "Tricky Dick" and "Slick Willy," it is little wonder that honesty and integrity are the exception and not the rule. But these values are still high on God's list, as their prominence in the book of Proverbs would indicate. Together they are a pearl every woman should value in the wardrobe of virtues.

## Understanding Honesty and Integrity

1. Look up the words "honesty" and "integrity" in your dictionary or a dictionary of synonyms. Define each word and note the difference between them.

Integrity keeps your eyes on your own paper during the test. Integrity makes you record and submit only true figures on your expense account. Integrity keeps your personal life pure and straight, regardless of the benefits and personal perks that might come your way through compromise.[1]

2. A related word in Proverbs is "upright." Look up this word in your dictionary, noting the definition that has to do with morality.

## Honest in Deed

3. Read Proverbs 11:1; 16:11; 20:10 and 23. What do these four verses teach us about being honest in our dealings?

*God detests dishonesty*

4. How does the concept of "weights and measures" apply to life today?

The story is told of the bus driver who collected a man's fare and gave back to him too much change. As the man was leaving the bus at his appointed stop, he returned the extra change to the bus driver. "I believe you gave me too much money," the passenger said. "I did it on purpose," said the driver. "I heard you preach yesterday, and I wanted to see if you lived like you talked."

5. According to Proverbs 28:6, when is being poor desirable?

*4 being blameless*

## A Biblical example

6. Read 2 Kings 12:1-16. Joash (also spelled Jehoash) was a young king of Judah. The people had been worshiping idols, and the temple of God had fallen into disrepair. (a) How was money collected to make the necessary repairs (v. 9)?

*as people were coming into the temple*

This money was then given to the foremen who oversaw the temple repairs so they could pay the workmen. (b) What remarkable statement is made about these foremen in verse 15? ("Faithfully" can also be translated "honestly.")

*they were so honest they didn't even need to keep an accounting of expenses*

## Honest in Speech

7. Read Proverbs 6:16-19 and 12:22. What does God hate, and in what does He delight?
*haughty eyes, one who stirs up dissension, lying tongue, hands that shed innocent blood, wicked scheming, rushing into evil*
*delights in truth*

8. Why do you think God expresses Himself so strongly about lying?

9. Read Revelation 21:27 and 22:15. Who will ultimately be excluded from God's presence?

*impure         magic                    liars*
*deceitful       sexually immoral*
*shameful       Murderers*
*idolators*

10. Read Ephesians 4:25. What was Paul's instruction to the Christians in Ephesus?   *don't lie, speak truth*

11. According to Proverbs 12:19, what is the contrast between telling the truth and lying?   *truthful lips last forever*
*lying tongue only a moment*

12. What warning is repeated two times in Proverbs 19:5 and 9?
*a liar will be punished*

13. Read Proverbs 21:6. What happens to the person who lies to get gain?   *It will not last*

## A Biblical example

14. Read the account of Ananias and Sapphira in Acts 5:1–10. (a) What dishonest thing did they do?

*they sold property, + pretended to give all of the proceeds to the church when really they kept some for themselves*

(b) How were they punished?

*death*

(c) They did not lie just to Peter and the apostles. Ultimately, to Whom did they lie?

*God*

## A Person of Integrity

A person who is honest in deed and word is worthy of trust; she is a person of integrity. Bridges points out that integrity begins by "living all of life in the conscious awareness of God's constant presence. And this should be a fundamental characteristic of the person who fears God."[2]

15. How does Proverbs 11:3 contrast the upright person and the person who is perverse? *the honest person's integrity guides him, whereas the person's integrity is destroyed by it*

16. Proverbs 10:9 also contrasts the person of integrity and the perverse person. What is the difference? *the person of integrity is secure in his behavior + his place w God whereas the person's integrity will be found out — not secure*

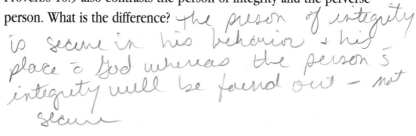

### A Biblical example

The Old Testament character Joseph is a sterling example of integrity. You can read his life story in chapters 37 and 39 through 50 of Genesis. His brothers hated him, so they sold him to merchants going to Egypt. He ultimately became a servant to an Egyptian captain, Potiphar.

17. How do we know Potiphar trusted Joseph (Genesis 39:4)?

*Put him in charge of his household*

Joseph was a handsome young man. At some point, Potiphar's wife decided she would have an affair with him. He repeatedly withstood her advances (39:7-10). Eventually she trapped him as he went about his duties.

18. How did Joseph maintain his integrity (39:11-13)?

*He did not give in to the wife — he did not accuse her of her lies*

Joseph was imprisoned for several years, but God did not forget him. Even in prison, Joseph acted with integrity. Because of his ability to interpret dreams and his leadership capabilities, Joseph was promoted by Pharaoh to be second in command in Egypt. But "the rest of the story" is that God used the events in Joseph's life to ultimately save his own family (see Genesis 50:20). What an example of an upright man who was guided by integrity!

In writing of Joseph's integrity, Swindoll says, "Make no mistake, integrity is tough stuff. Integrity does not take the easy way, make the easy choices, or choose the 'pleasures for a season' path. Above all, integrity is what you are when there isn't anyone around to check up on you; it's best demonstrated when nobody's watching."[3]

God places a high priority on honesty and integrity. Do you? Is this pearl part of your wardrobe?

> I want a principle within Of watchful, godly fear,
> A sensibility of sin, A pain to feel it near.
> Help me the first approach to feel Of pride or wrong desire,
> To catch the wand'ring of my will And quench the kindling fire.

Almighty God of truth and love, To me Thy pow'r impart;
The burden from my soul remove, The hardness from my
  heart.
O may the least omission pain My reawakened soul,
And drive me to that grace again Which makes the
  wounded whole.

—*Charles Wesley*

## Proverbs in Practice

1. You may not be tempted to be dishonest in major things, but you know that you "fudge" a little here and there. In what areas of life do you need to be on guard against dishonesty?

2. Why do people lie (apart from the fact that we all are born with a sin nature)? How can we teach our children to tell the truth—even though doing so may sometimes be hard and may lead to unpleasant results?

3. Ephesians 4:15 says we are to speak the truth in love. Why is this an important reminder? What happens when people do not speak the truth in love?

4. Integrity should be high on your list of desirable traits. Ask God to show you any areas of your life in which there is duplicity; ask Him each day to help you be a person of integrity.

## Proverbs in Prayer

*O God, there is no variableness or shadow of turning with You. You are truth. Honesty and integrity should characterize my life since I am Your child. You delight in honesty and hate lying. I want Your Spirit to reveal areas of duplicity in my life. Teach me that it is better to be poor and upright than rich and perverse. May I know the security, or surety, that comes from living an upright life. I pray this in the name of the Lord Jesus, amen.*

Notes

1. Charles Swindoll, *Joseph: A Man of Integrity and Forgiveness* (Nashville: Word Publishing, 1998), p. 179.

2. Bridges, *The Joy of Fearing God*, p. 180.

3. Swindoll, *Joseph*, p. 180.

# The Pearl of Diligence

*"The soul of the sluggard desireth, and hath nothing: but the soul of the diligent shall be made fat" (Proverbs 13:4).*

**D**id you ever learn the little couplet that says, "If a task is once begun, Never leave it 'till it's done; / Be it great or be it small, Do it well or not at all"? The essence of that couplet is diligence: sticking with something, or, as the dictionary defines it, "persevering application."

It is so easy to quit! We live in a society that starts lots of things it never finishes. Children easily give up if an activity loses its challenge or the game doesn't go the way they wanted it to go. Adults start projects and never finish them—sometimes because they lack the perseverance to see something through to the end. We live in an "instant" society—from food service to computer speed. Perhaps that contributes to our lack of diligence, our ability to see a task or project through to the end.

As we look at what the Bible teaches about diligence in the book of Proverbs, we will encounter two other words that are the opposite of diligence: lazy and sluggard.

1. Write the definitions of these words. Use your English dictionary for help.

   • Lazy

• Sluggard

## Diligence in Personal Habits

2. Read Proverbs 4:23-27. (a) What did Solomon say should be kept with diligence? *guard your heart*

(b) What do you think "heart" means in this verse?

*soul, it is who you are*

3. Why is it so important to "keep," or watch over, our hearts with diligence? Read Proverbs 4:23 again, along with Matthew 12:34 and 15:18 and 19. *you "express" whatever is in your heart - good or evil*

4. Read Proverbs 20:13. What is another characteristic of the diligent person? *not lazy*

5. Along with Proverbs 20:13, read 19:15 and 24:33 and 34. What did Solomon say happens to the person who loves sleep?

*lazy -
hunger
poverty
Scarcity*

6. How does this apply to life today?

*lazy person won't get what they need in life, won't be able to provide to others*

7. Read Proverbs 11:27. What happens to the person who diligently pursues good things? "Good things" are not the "good life" that we hear extolled today, but things that are morally upright and good.

*will find good*

This proverb is echoed today in the maxim "The hand that gives gathers."

8. Another personal habit of the diligent person is that she accepts responsibility for her actions. In contrast, read the following verses and note the excuses of the lazy person.

- Proverbs 22:13 *can't go out because there is danger when there is not*

- Proverbs 20:4 *doesnt do his work & so doesnt get his reward*

Excuses abound in our world! Making excuses will keep you from studying your Bible; they will keep you from memorizing Scripture. Making excuses will keep you from moving toward physical and spiritual fitness. Be diligent; persevere; don't rely on excuses!

Awake, my soul, and with the sun
Thy daily stage of duty run;
Shake off dull sloth, and joyful rise
To pay thy morning sacrifice.

Lord, I my vows to Thee renew;
Disperse my sins as morning dew:
Guard my first springs of thought and will,
And with Thyself my spirit fill.

Direct, control, suggest this day
All I design, or do, or say;
That all my powers, with all their might,
In Thy sole glory may unite.

*—Thomas Ken*

## Diligence in Work

9. According to Proverbs 18:9, what is true of the person who is slothful in his work?

*a brother to one who destroys*

10. Read Proverbs 12:11 and 28:19. What happens when a person diligently tills his land? *abundant food*

11. Since most of us don't till the land in order to provide food for our families, what is the principle of these verses that we need to apply today?

12. Read Proverbs 22:29. What is the reward for the person who is diligent in her work?

13. Recall an example, if possible, of someone whose diligent work did not go unrewarded.

14. Review this lesson's key verse, Proverbs 13:4. What is the ultimate reward for the diligent person?

*Desires of the diligent are fully satisfied*

## A Biblical Example

Perhaps one of the best examples of diligence in the Bible is found right in the book of Proverbs. Chapter 31 describes the "virtuous woman."

15. Describe this woman's diligence as noted in each of the following verses:

- verse 13 *She makes cloth linen out of wool + flax*

- verse 14 *going + getting food from afar for her family*

- verse 15 *gets up while still dark to provide food*

- verse 16 *buys a field + plants a vineyard*

- verse 17 *she works vigorously*

- verse 18 *trades profitably, doesn't let her lamp go out!*

- verses 19-21 *Spins thread helps the poor. Cloths her family*

- verse 27 *is not lazy watches over the affairs of her household*

16. As remarkable as this woman is, it is not her diligence or industriousness for which she is ultimately praised. Read verse 30. What is her crowning virtue? *fears the Lord*

If there is a Biblical woman we can seek to emulate, it is the virtuous woman of Proverbs 31. Along with all her other accomplishments, she wore well the pearl of diligence.

## Proverbs in Practice

1. What are some things you can do to "keep," or "watch over," your heart with diligence?

2. Why is diligence necessary in order to succeed in things like a course of study, a fitness program, a new hobby or craft, or other pursuits?

3. You may work outside the home, or your employment may be homemaker. Regardless of your workplace, in what areas do you need to exercise diligence?

4. Is it easier to be diligent in some areas than in others? Explain your answer.

## Proverbs in Prayer

*Dear Father, I confess that I do not always keep, or watch over, my heart, my inner being and mind, with diligence. I am so easily influenced by the things of this world. Help me be diligent in maintaining habits that please You. I do not want to be like the slothful person who makes dumb excuses for her lack of perseverance (like the man in Proverbs who never ventured out for fear of a lion in the street!). Above all, may I model my life after the virtuous woman of Proverbs 31. I ask these things in the name of the Lord Jesus, Who set His face like a flint, and went all the way to the Cross for me. Amen.*

L  E  S  S  O  N    6

# The Pearl of Self-control

*"He that is slow to anger is better than the mighty; and he that ruleth his spirit than he that taketh a city"* (Proverbs 16:32).

In 2 Timothy 3 the apostle Paul defined some of the characteristics that would be true of society as the world gets closer and closer to the time of the return of Christ. One of those characteristics is "without self-control" (the meaning of "incontinent" in verse 3).

In much the same way as our society lacks stick-to-itiveness, it also lacks the ability to say no. And that is precisely what self-control is: knowing when to say no. "It is the willpower not to act on impulse or not to indulge when you know you shouldn't."[1]

In this study we will look at four areas in which we need to exercise self-control.

## Control at the Table

Of great interest to many women is what Proverbs teaches about what we eat.

1. Read Proverbs 25:16 and 27. What principle is taught in these two verses? *Eat just enough – not too much*

49

2. Read Proverbs 23:1-3. (a) What picture did Solomon use to suggest not overeating? *put a knife to your throat instead*

   (b)  The context of this verse deals with more than just overeating. What is the setting?

      *dining c̄ a ruler*

   (c)  What do you think Solomon had in mind?

      *the ruler wants to influence you c̄ his delicacies*

3. Read Proverbs 23:20 and 21. What is the command in these verses?

      *don't eat or drink too much — to excess*

We often take on the habits of the people with whom we associate. Solomon's counsel was to practice self-control sooner rather than later. It is better not to be in the presence of drinkers and gluttons than to try to restrain ourselves in their presence.

   4. Read Proverbs 23:29-34. What is another area in which we must exercise self-control?

      *c̄ alcohol*

> These verses present the longest and most articulate warning in Proverbs against drunkenness. . . . Six questions call attention to emotional problems, . . . social problems, . . . and physical problems . . . that stem from lingering long over wine and mixed wine. . . . Wine seems attractive . . . but eventually it is as devastating and painful as a snake bite.[2]

## A Biblical example

5. A Biblical example of self-control in regard to food and drink is the four Hebrew children. Read Daniel 1:3-16. (a) What did the king want the four young men to eat?

*the kings food - the 1st portion had been offered to idols + ceremonially unclean animals were used*

(b) What did Daniel say he would be doing if he ate these things?

*defile himself*

(c) Daniel had the self-control to say no to things he knew he should not eat. What was the outcome?

*they looked healthier + God gave them knowledge + understanding*

## Control of Our Tongues

Not only do we need to exercise tongue-control at the table; we also need to exercise tongue-control in relation to our speech.

6. According to Proverbs 11:12 and 17:28, what does a person of understanding do? *holds his tongue*

7. Read Proverbs 10:19. What is true of a person who "refraineth [her] lips"? *wise*

8. Give some examples of times when using self-control and saying nothing is better than speaking.

9. Read Proverbs 21:23. What is true of the person who guards her tongue (or practices self-control in regard to speech)?

*keeps himself from Calamity*

10. If we practice this verse (Proverbs 21:23) in our homes, what results could we expect to see?

Solomon had much more to say about speech and the tongue; that is the subject of study in lesson 9. But one other text is important in regard to control of the tongue.

11. Read James 3:2-10. What is James's conclusion about the tongue in verse 8?

*no man can tame the tongue, it is a restless evil, full of deadly poison*

Control of the tongue is humanly impossible. Self-control is a fruit of the Spirit (Galatians 5:22, 23), and only with the help of the Holy Spirit can we learn to control our tongues.

## Control of Our Tempers

12. Review Proverbs 16:32. To what is the person compared who can control her temper?

*Better to control temper than to be a warrior*

13. Read Proverbs 25:28. To what is the person compared who cannot control her temper?

*like a city whose walls are broken down*

14. According to Proverbs 14:29, what is true of the quick-tempered person?  *foolish*

15. Give some examples of the "folly" a quick-tempered person may encounter.  *road rage. broken equipment broken relationship sin*

16. Read Proverbs 19:11. The meaning of "glory" is honor. According to this verse, what is honorable? *to overlook an offense*

> Outbursts of temper are harmful not only because they release our own ungoverned, sinful passions, but more importantly because they wound those who are the recipients of such outbursts. . . . To have a temper that requires control is not a mark of ungodliness; to fail to control it is. To succeed, by God's grace, in controlling an unruly temper is to demonstrate godly self-control. [3]

## Control of Our Thoughts

Bridges points out that "the battle for self-control is fought primarily within our own minds."[4]

17. Read 2 Corinthians 10:5. What did Paul say we should do with our thoughts? *take captive every thought & make it obedient to Christ*

18. Read Proverbs 23:7. Why are thoughts so important?

19. Proverbs 6:16-18 lists seven things that God hates. Which one of them relates to thoughts?

*a heart that devises wicked schemes*

20. Philippians 4:8 gives us a list of things to think about. Write them here. *True, noble, right, pure, lovely, admirable, excellent, praiseworthy*

> Take Thou our minds, dear Lord, we humbly pray;
> Give us the mind of Christ each passing day;
> Teach us to know the truth that sets us free;
> Grant us in all our thoughts to honor Thee.
>
> Take Thou our wills, Most High! hold Thou full sway;
> Have in our inmost souls Thy perfect way;
> Guard Thou each sacred hour from selfish ease;
> Guide Thou our ordered lives as Thou dost please.
> —*William H. Foulkes*

We do not gain Heaven by practicing self-control. But true followers of Jesus Christ will evidence their devotion to Him by allowing the Holy Spirit to cultivate the pearl of self-control in their lives.

## Proverbs in Practice

1. If self-control at the table is a problem for you, consider these questions: Do you have more trouble exercising self-control at the table when

you eat alone or when you eat with others? How can you figuratively "put a knife to your throat" in order to exercise self-control?

2. In what kinds of situations do you find tongue-control to be most difficult? What steps can you take to practice more self-control at these times?

3. Do you have a short fuse? Ask God to help you exercise control over your temper.

4. What kinds of things affect what we think about? We need to guard the gates to our minds!

5. Jerry Bridges observes that "the battle of self-control is different for each of us."[5] Does some area of your life control you rather than your controlling it? Juanita Purcell, in her book on the fruit of the Spirit, gives these questions; if you answer yes to one or more of them, you need to ask God for the strength to practice self-control.
   • Are you trying to hide something you are doing?
   • Are you making excuses for what you are doing by blaming others or circumstances for your lack of control in this area of your life?
   • Do you continue to do this even though you have repeatedly tried to stop?
   • Do you say, "I can stop whenever I want to," even while you continue to do it?
   • Do you cover up this area of your life by lying about it?
   • Are you continuing a habit that you know does not please the Lord?[6]

## Proverbs in Prayer

*O Lord, I long to be a person who rules my own spirit. I do not want to be like a city with broken walls; such a condition leaves me more vulnerable to Satan's attacks. Help me to bring my thought-life into captivity. It is so easy to think that thoughts don't matter, that they are private, that I can "get away" with thoughts that do not please You. But Your Word teaches me that this is not so. What I think, I am. In all areas of my life, may I yield to the Holy Spirit, Who alone can produce the fruit of self-control. In the name of Your Son I pray, amen.*

### Notes

1. Juanita Purcell, *Be Patient—I'm Not Perfect Yet* (Schaumburg, Ill.: Regular Baptist Press, 1993), p. 94.

2. Walvoord and Zuck, p. 957.

3. Bridges, *The Practice of Godliness*, p. 172.

4. Bridges, *The Practice of Godliness*, p. 175.

5. Bridges, *The Practice of Godliness*, p. 174.

6. Purcell, p. 98.

# The Pearl of Friendship

*"A friend loveth at all times, and a brother is born for adversity" (Proverbs 17:17).*

I f you have enjoyed any of the Anne of Green Gables books, you know that Anne, an orphan girl being brought up by a spinster sister and bachelor brother (unrelated to Anne), longed for a friend. "Marilla," Anne asked, "do you think that I shall ever have a bosom friend in Avonlea?" Marilla was quite shocked at Anne's choice of words, but Anne went on to explain: "A bosom friend—an intimate friend, you know—a really kindred spirit to whom I can confide my inmost soul." When Anne found Diana, she found her bosom friend, her kindred spirit. Through thick and thin (and there was plenty of both!), Anne and Diana remained true friends.

What comes to your mind when you hear the word "friend"? Or perhaps the better question is, Who comes to mind? Maybe you recall childhood or school friends. Some people stay in touch with those friends for many years. But the friendships we form as adults are probably the ones we cherish the most. The dictionary says a friend is "one attached to another by affection or esteem." Luci Swindoll says friendship is "one of life's most valuable gifts."[1] Solomon must have thought friendship was valuable, for he devoted a good number of proverbs to the subject.

## Establishing Good Relationships

Some people complain that they have no friends. People who say this often make little attempt to be friendly. Take stock of your own life. If you feel that you do not have friends, ask God to help you reach out and befriend someone else. You may be surprised. Sometimes friends are found in unlikely places!

1. Read Proverbs 13:20. What does this verse suggest about establishing relationships? *choose your friends č care*

2. (a)  What imagery is suggested in Proverbs 27:17?

*one person "sharpening" another —*

(b)  How does this apply to friendship?

*taking care, developing*

## Avoiding Bad Relationships

Solomon had as much or more to say about avoiding bad relationships as he did about establishing good ones.

3. Read Proverbs 22:24 and 25. (a) What kind of relationship should be avoided? *relationship č a hot-tempered person*

(b)  Why?

*because you may become like him*

4. Read Proverbs 20:19. (a) What kind of person should be avoided according to this verse? *a gossip*

(b) Why do you think Solomon gave this warning?
*because that friend will talk about you*

5. Proverbs 23:20 and 21 and 28:7 refer to another relationship to avoid. (a) What is it? *drunks + gluttons*

(b) What is gluttony? *eating too much*

(c) What character trait that we have already studied in Proverbs is the opposite of gluttony? *self control*

6. According to Proverbs 24:1 and 2, what is yet another relationship to avoid? *wicked men*

7. Read Proverbs 19:4 and 6 and 14:20. What do you think these verses teach about friendships? *false friends will follow after money but not be true friends*

8. The prodigal son in the story Jesus told is a good example of this
   kind of relationship. Read Luke 15:11-15 with the thought in mind
   that the prodigal's "riotous living" included companions. What
   happened when the young man's money ran out?

   *he worked for other people*

## Being a Good Friend

Luci Swindoll says, "Be good to your friends! Give them your time and
interest. Listen to their problems. Enter into their joys. Work through
your difficulties in every way possible. Be faithful and involved."[2] Many of
those same ideas are found in Proverbs.

9. Read Proverbs 11:13, 16:28, and 17:9. What do these verses teach
   about being a good friend? *Don't gossip, keep
   your friends secrets,
   forgive*

10. What does a friend do according to Proverbs 17:17?

    *loves @ all-time*

11. Proverbs 27:6 talks about the "wounds of a friend" as being faithful.
    What do you think this means?

    *they will tell you what you need
    to hear (?)*

12. What characteristic of friendship is described in Proverbs 27:9?

*like perfume they bring joy*

## A Biblical Example

One of the best examples of true friendship in the Bible is the relationship between David and Jonathan.

13. Who was David (1 Samuel 16:1, 4-13)?

14. Who was Jonathan (1 Samuel 14:1 and 13:1)?

*Son of Saul*

15. After David killed Goliath (1 Samuel 17), the relationship between David and Jonathan developed. They were an unlikely pair: a shepherd boy and a king's son. Describe their friendship after you read 1 Samuel 18:1-4. *they were best friends, like brothers*

Saul became extremely jealous of David and sought to kill him. First Samuel 19:1-7 records one time Jonathan saved David's life; chapter 20 records another time. Finally David had to flee.

16. Read 1 Samuel 20:41 and 42 and describe the parting of David and Jonathan. *sad*

17. Review the characteristics of a good friend in questions 10-13. Which of these characteristics were true of David and Jonathan?

Charles Swindoll describes the relationship between David and Jonathan as an "intimate friendship." Then he gives four characteristics of this kind of friendship.

> Intimate friends are rare in life. Often we have only one, occasionally two . . . usually not more than three in our entire lives. There's something about an intimate friend that causes your souls to be knit together. It's what we call a kindred spirit. Intimate friendship has four characteristics, and we find all of them in this story [David and Jonathan]. First, an intimate friend is willing to sacrifice. . . . Second, an intimate friend is a loyal defense before others. . . . Third, intimate friends give each other complete freedom to be themselves. . . . And finally, an intimate friend is a constant source of encouragement.[3]

## The Ultimate Friendship

When Solomon wrote about "a friend that sticketh closer than a brother" (Proverbs 18:24), he may well have had in mind divine friendship. Truly, the only One Who can stick with us through thick and thin is the Lord Jesus Himself. Jesus calls us His friends if we do what He commands (John 15:14). The starting place for that obedience is to recognize that the only way to God is through Jesus Christ, Who is the way, the truth, and life (John 14:6). Have you received the Lord Jesus as your Savior? Are you His child and friend (John 1:12)?

> I've found a Friend, O such a Friend!
> He loved me ere I knew Him;
> He drew me with the cords of love,
> And thus He bound me to Him. . . .

I've found a Friend, O such a Friend!
He bled, He died to save me;
And not alone the gift of life,
But His own self He gave me. . . .

I've found a Friend, O such a Friend!
So kind and true and tender,
So wise a Counselor and Guide,
So mighty a Defender!
From Him who loves me now so well,
What pow'r my soul can sever?
Shall life or death, or earth or hell?
No! I am His forever.

*—James G. Small*

## Proverbs in Practice

1. If you have children, how can you help them establish good relationships and avoid bad ones?


2. Based on what you studied about establishing good relationships and being a good friend, write a description of what you understand true friendship to be.


3. Luci Swindoll points out that "friendship has to be reciprocal—a give and take arrangement of nurturing and growing together."[4] What are you doing to nurture the friendships in your life?


4. Take time to thank God for a special, or intimate, friend. Do something for that friend as soon as possible: send a card, make a phone call,

deliver a basket of freshly baked muffins, go to lunch, buy her some flowers, or do something else your friend will enjoy.

5. Do you know the Lord Jesus as your friend? What are you doing to nurture that relationship?

### Proverbs in Prayer

*Dear Father, help me to choose my friends wisely. May the relationships I establish honor You. Help me to be friendly to others. Help me be a faithful friend, keeping my mouth shut when that is appropriate and opening it in praise, encouragement, and counsel when that is called for. Thank You for the Lord Jesus, the Friend Who sticks closer than a brother. I pray these things in His name, amen.*

Notes

1. Luci Swindoll, *Wide My World, Narrow My Bed* (Portland, Ore.: Multnomah Press, 1982), p. 119.

2. Luci Swindoll, pp. 134, 135.

3. Charles Swindoll, *David: A Man of Passion and Destiny* (Dallas: Word Publishing, 1997), pp. 52-54.

4. Luci Swindoll, p. 127.

# The Pearl of a Happy Home

*"My son, hear the instruction of thy father, and forsake
not the law of thy mother" (Proverbs 1:8).*

W hat's happening to our homes?" is a frequent question these
days. As politicians, educators, clergy, psychologists, and everyone else involved in the debate of what has happened to America's kids
ponder the issues, the home comes under increasing attack. It's an age-
old problem, as old as the early chapters of Genesis. Remember, the first
murder was one sibling killing another sibling. But there is help!

A friend of mine was once asked for her recommendation of good
books on child-rearing. She said she and her husband had used only one
book: the book of Proverbs. On the surface, that may seem like a simplis-
tic answer. But look a little deeper. Probably no other book of the Bible
has as much to say about men and women, parents and children. God is
vitally concerned about homes and families; after all, they were His idea
in the first place! One of the priceless pearls of Proverbs is its rich teaching on the home.

## The Home

1. Read Proverbs 24:3 and 4. What makes a strong home?

*wisdom understanding + knowledge*

2. Read Proverbs 15:17 and 17:1. What two qualities are more desirable in a home than prosperity? *love + peace*

Many people have found that a home where material possessions are few but love for each other is present is far better than a house of great opulence where people hate each other. Love makes one's difficult circumstances endurable, whereas hatred undoes all the enjoyments that good food might otherwise bring.[1]

3. Read Proverbs 12:7 and 14:11. What kind of home endures?

*righteous*
*upright*

## Husbands and Wives

4. According to Proverbs 5:15-19, what should be a husband's attitude toward his wife? *be faithful*

5. Read Proverbs 31:28. What did the husband of the virtuous woman do publicly? *praise her*

6. How does praising family members contribute to a happy home?

7. What is a wife called in Proverbs 18:22?

*good*

8. Read Proverbs 31:11 and 12. When men and women fulfill their Biblical roles in a marriage and home, what is the outcome?

*they have all they need*

9. How does Proverbs 12:4 describe a virtuous woman?

*her husband's crown*

10. While Proverbs 31:10-31 describes the virtuous wife and mother, some other proverbs deal with the less-than-ideal wife and mother. Read Proverbs 21:9, 21:19, and 25:24. Summarize the "it is better to ... than ..." teaching of these verses.

*don't want to live i a quarrelsome wife*

11. What is the woman's problem in Proverbs 27:15 and 19:13?

*quarrelsome — constant dripping — annoying*

## Parents and Children

12. What responsibility do parents have according to Proverbs 22:6?

*Train a child in the way he should go*

In Proverbs 22:6, *hanak* [the Hebrew word for "train"] means to limit, narrow, focus, or "hedge in" the child's conduct in godly directions. To *hanak* a structure

was to limit, narrow, or specify its use. Every child is to be
started in the right direction morally.[2]

13. Many proverbs relate to the correction, or discipline, of children.
Note what each of the following verses says about this subject.

- Proverbs 13:24 *he who loves is careful to discipline Spares the rod, hates the child*

- Proverbs 23:13 *do not withhold discipline*

- Proverbs 19:18 *discipline to provide hope, prevent death*

- Proverbs 22:15 *discipline gets rid of folly*

- Proverbs 29:15 *rod of correction imparts wisdom*

- Proverbs 29:17 *discipline + he will give you peace*

The Bible approves of physical punishment. However,
these verses in no way justify harsh, extreme, or unreason-
able physical punishment of a child. The discipline should
be carefully suited to the misbehavior, and should be given
in love, not hate. . . . The rod is to be applied because of
the child's folly or foolishness. . . . However, folly in the
Bible does not mean silliness or lightheartedness. Instead,
it connotes a wicked, sinful heart, or the opposite of godliness. . . . Therefore, physical punishment is to be limited
to children's persistence in sinful, God-defying actions.[3]

14. Children have a responsibility to heed and respond to the instruction given by their parents. What is the result when children obey
Proverbs 1:8? Each of the following verses gives a result. *listen to parents*

- Proverbs 2:1, 5 *listen to teaching to understand fear of God + find knowledge of God*

• Proverbs 3:1, 2 *bring prosperity*

• Proverbs 4:20-22 *pay attention, listen closely — bring health*

• Proverbs 6:20, 22 *guidance, watch over you speak to you*

• Proverbs 23:24, 25 *parental joy*

15. In contrast to the good results noted above, what is true of the foolish child?

• Proverbs 15:20 *despises his mother*

• Proverbs 17:25 *grief to father, bitterness to mother*

• Proverbs 19:27 *stray from words of knowledge*

## A Biblical Example

16. The Old Testament book of Ruth is a story about families. Who were the members of the first family described in the account (Ruth 1:2)?

*Elimelech, Ruth Mahlon Kilion*

17. After the death of Naomi's husband, whom did her sons marry (Ruth
1:3, 4)? *Moabite women – Orpah & Ruth*

We don't know the number of years that passed between events in
Ruth 1, but we read that eventually Naomi's two sons died, leaving her in
a foreign land with her daughters-in-law. You may know the story. Naomi
decided to return to Israel, and daughter-in-law Ruth went with her.
Through a wonderful series of events, in which we see the providence of
God in the lives of these women, Ruth married Boaz. (Read chapters 2
and 3.)

18. Describe the family scene in Ruth 4:13-16.

*happy*

19. How was Ruth's child related to Solomon, the writer of Proverbs?
*Son – Obed – son Jesse – Son David son – Solomon*

What a difference it would make in our churches, communities, and
country if husbands and wives, parents and children lived according to
the wisdom of Proverbs! You can't change other people's homes, but you
can work on your own. Ask God to help you cultivate the pearl of a
happy home according to Biblical standards.

> Happy the home when God is there,
> And love fills every breast,
> When one their wish and one their prayer
> And one their heav'nly rest.
>
> Happy the home where Jesus' name
> Is sweet to every ear,
> Where children early lisp His fame
> And parents hold Him dear.

Happy the home where prayer is heard
And praise is wont to rise,
Where parents love the sacred Word
And all its wisdom prize.

Lord, let us in our homes agree
This blessed peace to gain;
Unite our hearts in love to Thee,
And love to all will reign.

*—Henry Ware, Jr.*

## Proverbs in Practice

1. Listen to mealtimes in your home. Are they characterized by love and peace? If not, what steps can you take to change things?

2. Read Proverbs 31:10-31 every day for a week. Paraphrase some of these characteristics in your own words. Ask God to help you develop these traits in your life.

3. Do you practice godly correction and discipline in your home?

4. What steps are you taking to train your children in godly ways?

5. How can godly grandparents influence their grandchildren?

6. Perhaps you live alone or live with another gal. How can you have a happy home?

## Proverbs in Prayer

*Heavenly Father, help me to recognize that You established the home and the principles that make a happy home. I do not want to be a brawling, contentious, or angry woman. Regardless of my age or marital status, help me make the place I live a place where You are honored. In Jesus' name I pray, amen.*

Notes
1. Walvoord and Zuck, p. 938.
2. Roy Zuck, *Precious in His Sight* (Grand Rapids: Baker Books, 1996), p. 135.
3. Zuck, p. 123.

# The Pearl of Wholesome Speech

*"He that keepeth his mouth keepeth his life: but he that openeth wide his lips shall have destruction" (Proverbs 13:3).*

When I was a child, it was not uncommon to hear these words on the playground: "Sticks and stones may break my bones, but words will never hurt me." The idea behind this recitation was to deflect another child's angry words, pretending that they were of no concern at all. But was it true? Probably even the children knew it was not. Words may not break bones, but they certainly have the power to crush one's spirit, lower one's self-esteem, and break one's heart. Oh, the negative effect of words!

But words can also encourage, build up, and give life. Words can be used to rouse people to action, to comfort people who grieve, to instruct people in right ways. Oh, the positive effect of words!

Perhaps no other single subject receives as much attention in Proverbs as our speech. Obviously, control of the tongue is an age-old problem. Wholesome speech must have been as rare in Solomon's day as it is in ours. A good summary statement on the tongue is Proverbs 18:21: "Death and life are in the power of the tongue." To better understand what Proverbs teaches about speech, we will look first at the unwholesome use of words and then at the wholesome use of words.

## Unwholesome Use of Words

### Gossip

1. What is gossip?

2. Is gossip always false? Explain your answer.

3. Read Proverbs 16:28 and 17:9. What happens to a friendship if one person gossips?

   Separates

4. Read Proverbs 18:8. The word "wounds" can be translated "choice morsels." How does this verse help you understand why people like to share and listen to gossip?

   they seen good to hear, but they stick to you + impact how you feel + act toward the person

5. Not only should we not gossip ourselves, but, according to Proverbs 20:19, what else should be true of us?

   stay away from a gossip since they will betray your confidence

### Lying

We dealt with lying in more detail in lesson 4. You may want to review pages 35 and 36, "Honest in Speech."

6. Read Proverbs 6:16 and 17. Of the things God hates, which ones apply to speech? *lying*

7. Review your answer to question 8 in lesson 4 (p. 35). Why is lying so detestable to God?

8. According to Proverbs 13:5, what does a righteous person hate? *what is false*

9. Read Proverbs 17:7, Lying is particularly unbecoming to what person? *a ruler*

### Flattery

10. What is flattery? How is it related to lying?

11. Read Proverbs 26:28. To what does flattery lead?

*ruin*

12. Read Proverbs 29:5. What happens to a person who flatters?

13. According to Proverbs 28:23, what is more beneficial in the long run than flattery? *rebuke*

## Corrupt speech

14. What command is found in Proverbs 4:24?

*Keep corrupt talk from your lips*

15. What kinds of speech could be considered "corrupt talk"?

*foul language*
*lying derisive*

16. Read Proverbs 17:20. (a) What happens to the person who has a perverse, or corrupt, tongue? *falls into trouble*

(b) What do you think this means?

The book of Proverbs deals with other kinds of unwholesome speech. To further study this subject, trace these topics in Proverbs: quarreling, bearing false witness, boasting, slandering.

## Wholesome Use of Words

### True words

17. Read Proverbs 12:17, 19, and 22. What do these verses teach us about the importance of true words?

*truthful lips last forever*
*Lord delights in truthful men*

### Appropriate words

18. (a) What kind of words are described in Proverbs 10:32?

*fitting*

(b) Give an example of this kind of speech.

19. How are fitting, or appropriate, words described in Proverbs 15:1, and what is the result of using them?

*turn away anger*

20. What kind of speech is encouraged in Proverbs 15:23, and what does it do? *timely - joy*

21. Recall a time when you were the recipient of "a word spoken in due season."

22. Read Proverbs 16:24. What is the value of pleasant words?

Sweet to the soul
+ healing to the bones

23. What is the picture of appropriate words in Proverbs 25:11?

apples of gold in a setting of silver

**Helpful, encouraging words**

24. Read Proverbs 12:25. (a) What does a good word do for a person?

cheers him up

(b) When has someone's good or kind word had this effect on you?

25. Proverbs 10:11 describes the mouth of the righteous person as a "well [or fountain] of life." What does this word picture suggest to you? overflowing i positive comments

26. (a) In contrast to reckless words that hurt, what does Proverbs 12:18 say about the tongue of the wise?

*brings healing*

(b) What kinds of healing could be in view here?

*heart emotions*

Other types of wholesome words in Proverbs include wise words, few words, and carefully chosen words. You may want to study these themes in the book of Proverbs. What lovely pearls are wholesome words!

## A Biblical Example

"In the beginning was the Word, and the Word was with God, and the Word was God. . . . And the Word was made flesh, and dwelt among us, (and we beheld his glory, the glory as of the only begotten of the Father,) full of grace and truth" (John 1:1, 14). As the Word, the Lord Jesus is our supreme example in the wholesome use of words.

27. Describe the words of Christ in each of the following Scripture passages.

• Luke 4:22  *gracious words*

• Matthew 7:29  *taught c̄ authority*

• Mark 10:16  *blessed the children*

• John 8:11 *did not condem*

• John 14:1 *reassuring*

## Guarding Our Mouths

28. According to Solomon, why should we guard our mouths (Proverbs 13:3 and 21:23)? *guards our lives protects self from calamity*

29. Read Proverbs 29:20. What will help us avoid unwholesome words and use wholesome words? *Do not speak in haste*

30. Read the words of Solomon's father, David, in Psalm 141:3. Write this prayer in your own words.

*Help me to speak carefully, slowly uplifting*

If all that we say,
In a single day
With never a word left out,
Were printed each night
In clear black and white,
T'would prove queer reading, no doubt.

And then, just suppose,
Ere our eyes we could close,
We must read the whole record through.

Then wouldn't we sigh
And wouldn't we try
A great deal less talking to do?

And I more than half think,
That many a kink
Would be smoother in life's tangled thread,
If half that we say,
In a single day,
Were left forever unsaid.

*—Unknown*

Ask God to help you cultivate the pearl of wholesome speech!

## Proverbs in Practice

1. If you have a tendency to gossip about other people, you need to ask God to help you control your tongue and give you victory in this area. What practical things can you do if someone wants to share gossip with you?

2. What can you do to avoid having to listen to corrupt, or dirty, speech?

3. If you have trouble finding the right words to use to encourage a friend or acquaintance in person, what can you do?

4. This study has covered several areas of speech, both negative and positive. What are one or two particular areas you need to work on? What steps can you take to make progress in these areas?

## Proverbs in Prayer

*O God, I admit before You that the power of the tongue is awesome for good or ill. I want my words to honor You. I want them to be like beautiful gold apples in silver settings. Help me keep my tongue from things that displease You: gossip, lying, flattery, and corrupt speech. Such words are sin. May I follow the example of Your Son, the Word You sent to earth, Who spoke gracious words. Help me guard my words, and in so doing, guard my life. These words I pray in the name of the Word, amen.*

# The Pearl of Sound Financial Management

*"Remove far from me vanity and lies: give me neither poverty nor riches; feed me with food convenient for me: Lest I be full, and deny thee, and say, Who is the LORD? or lest I be poor, and steal, and take the name of my God in vain" (Proverbs 30:8, 9).*

W e live in a materialistic society. Most of us, at sometime or another, get caught up in the pursuit of "things." And "things" cost money. But our society has found a way around the need for money, namely, credit. And so people find it relatively easy to spend beyond their means. But eventually that catches up with a person.

Mary Hunt is a case in point. She and her husband amassed $100,000 in credit card debt in their pursuit of the "things" they thought would make their lives complete. Eventually they were forced to give up many of those things, and they were on the brink of financial disaster. Mary started writing a newsletter, *Cheapskate Monthly,* to help herself and other people practice responsible spending. She has written several books, including *The Financially Confident Woman* (©1996, Broadman & Holman Publishers) and *The Complete Cheapskate* (©1997, Focus on the Family). Mary's story, to one degree or another, could probably be told by hundreds of thousands of people. The principles that worked for Mary and for others in her situation are found in God's Word. The good news is that we can practice those principles and avoid the pitfalls of unsound financial management. No book of the Bible more clearly presents these principles than the book of Proverbs.

## Making Money

1. What do Proverbs 10:4 and 13:4 and 11 suggest about the way we should make money? *diligent hands bring wealth desires of the diligent are fully satisfied*

2. What do Proverbs 10:2 and 13:11 teach about how not to get money? *Ill-gotten treasures are of no value*

   *Dishonest money dwindles away*

3. What are some ways people try to make money that fit the description in the verses mentioned above? *gambling   stealing   lying   embezzlement*

4. Read Proverbs 1:19. What happens to the person who is "greedy of gain"? *it will take your life*

5. According to Proverbs 21:5, what does the diligent person do that helps her have the money she needs? *plans*

   Setting goals is a practice God encourages His children to follow. Not that we should be overly specific and unalterably tied to our goals, thereby possibly missing God's will for us. But the call for aim in life is clear. . . . Without goals, we cannot be godly stewards.[1]

6. Review Proverbs 30:8 and 9 and read 23:4. (a) How much money should we seek to have? *give me enough to sustain me, not too little + not too much*

(b) What are the dangers of having too much or too little money?

*too much - disown God*
*too little steal + dishonor God's name*

7. Read Proverbs 15:16. What does this verse teach about the amount of money we should seek to have? *- enough - too much brings turmoil*

## Managing Money

8. Read the second part of Proverbs 22:7. What principle of money management does this verse suggest? *borrowing money makes you a servant to the lender*

> Debt puts you in bondage to people and institutions who have only their profit—not yours—in mind. But you know that God has your best interests at heart. And being His servant is true freedom indeed.[2]

9. Several verses in Proverbs indicate that the wise and righteous person is prosperous. (See 3:16; 8:18, 21; 14:24; 15:6; 22:4.) Since we know that righteous people are not generally among the wealthy

*wisdom → long life, riches, honor*
*those who seek God find riches, honor enduring wealth + prosperity, Fear of Lord - wealth, honor life*

people of the world (and since Christians in some parts of the world are extremely poor), what do you think is the principle taught in these verses?

Consider the things money *cannot* do: Money can buy a bed, but not sleep; books, but not brains; food, but not an appetite; cosmetics and clothes, but not beauty; a house, but not a home; doctors and medicine, but not health; luxuries, but not culture; religion, but not a Savior; a church, but not Heaven.

10. (a) What principle of money management is found in Proverbs 13:22? *Store up money as an inheritance for heirs*

(b) A common bumper sticker sported by retired people says, "We're spending our children's inheritance." Is this a Biblical attitude? Explain your answer. *no*

## Spending Money

11. What principle of using money is taught in Proverbs 3:9?

*Honor the Lord ē your wealth giving him the firstfruits – tithe – its all Gods anyhow*

I give to God because I love Him and because I am grateful beyond belief for all that He has done for me every day of my life. Giving from a grateful heart and expecting nothing in return is a sweet offering to the One who owns everything I have anyway. It's the very least I can do. And as I give I experience God's grace.[3]

Take my silver and my gold—
Not a mite would I withhold;
Take my intellect and use
Every pow'r as Thou shalt choose,
Every pow'r as Thou shalt choose.

*—Frances Ridley Havergal*

12. Read Proverbs 3:27 and 28. What else should we do with our money as we are able? *give to those in need*

13. (a) What paradox is presented in Proverbs 11:24-26?

*give & you will be given hold onto what you have & you will become poor*

(b) In Acts 20:35 Paul quoted the words of Jesus Christ. How do they relate to the principle you just discovered in Proverbs?

*It is more blessed to give than to receive*

14. (a) According to Proverbs 19:17, giving to the poor is ultimately giving to Whom? *giving to God – who will reward you*

(b) Read Matthew 25:34-40. How did Jesus "flesh out" the truth of our giving to Him? *whenever you gave to the least of my brothers you gave to me*

## Warnings about Money

15. Review Proverbs 15:17 and 17:1. What is better in a home than great riches? *better to have basic food + love then great food c hatred + strife*

16. What else is more valuable than riches? Read Proverbs 16:8 and 28:6. *righteousness*

17. According to Proverbs 21:6-8, what kind of riches should be avoided? *those obtained by lying, violence*

18. Review Proverbs 30:8 and 9 again. What is the warning in these verses? *give me just enough so I don't disown the Lord or bring dishonor on his name*

## Biblical Examples

19. Skim Genesis 41:1-36. What principle concerning the management of assets do you learn from this account? *Cain brought God the 1st fruits - Abel's sacrifice was not sufficient    store up for hard times*

20. Read the parable of the talents in Matthew 25:14-29. What stewardship principle is illustrated in the parable? *invest your talents + your finances wisely or they will be taken from you*

21. (a) Read 2 Corinthians 8:2. How did the Macedonians practice the
principle of Proverbs 11:24-26? (See question 13.)

*they gave out of joy in spite of their poverty*

(b) Before they gave their money, what had the Macedonians done
(2 Corinthians 8:4, 5)?

*gave to God 1st*

22. (a) Read Philippians 4:14-19. What had the Philippian Christians
done for Paul? *Sent him aid again + again*

(b) What was his promise to them (v. 19)?
*God will meet all of their needs*

If you are practicing good financial management, then this pearl is already in your possession. If your money manages you more often than
you manage your money, you need to begin today to cultivate the pearl
of sound financial management. Since God's Word says so much about
money, you can be sure that God is willing to help you as you seek to apply these principles from Proverbs.

## Proverbs in Practice

1. What is your philosophy of money? In other words, what do you believe about money? How you behave with your money is an outgrowth of your belief. Write down your thoughts on this subject.

2. What are your short-term and long-term financial goals?

3. In what ways do you "honour the LORD" with your money?

4. Money is one of the leading causes of marital discord. If you are married, do you and your husband agree on money management? How can the principles in this lesson help you work toward financial harmony?

5. How can you teach financial responsibility to your children?

## Proverbs in Prayer

*Dear God, I recognize that everything I have comes from You. You have called me to manage these assets in a way that honors You. I would ask to be neither rich nor poor. I do not want to become self-sufficient and forget You; nor do I want to be poor and dishonor You. Help me to realize that I really am rich in things that money cannot buy. But You have entrusted me with money. Help me to give to those in need and to Your work. May I evidence godly wisdom in the way I make money, manage money, and spend money. I pray these things in the name of Your Son, Who was rich but became poor for my sake. Amen.*

Notes

1. Ron Blue, *Master Your Money Devotional Book* (Atlanta: Walk Thru the Bible Ministries, 1990), p. 12.

2. Blue, p. 19.

3. Mary Hunt, *The Financially Confident Woman* (Nashville: Broadman & Holman Publishers, 1996), p. 74.

# Conclusion

*"A wise man will hear, and will increase learning; and
a man of understanding shall attain unto wise counsels"
(Proverbs 1:5).*

I said in the preface to this study that the truths of Proverbs remind
me of a string of lovely pearls: one proverb after another is strung together to make the whole. I have also used the imagery of pearls because
I think most women like jewelry. We know that a well-chosen piece of
jewelry is an asset to our overall appearance. Just as a piece of jewelry
can enhance our physical appearance, so any of these "pearls" from Proverbs—these traits, virtues, truths—will enhance us spiritually, emotion-
ally, socially. These pearls for the inner woman will never go out of date;
the string will not break and scatter the jewels. You can wear them time
and again without apology.

So as we conclude this study in the book of Proverbs, each of us must
ask, "What am I going to do with what I have learned?" Solomon said a
wise person hears and adds to her learning. I have tried to suggest some
ways to put into practice the truths we have looked at in this practical,
down-to-earth Biblical book. I believe what James said centuries ago: we
deceive ourselves if we hear the Word but do not do it (James 1:22).

The key to obeying the Word of God goes back to fearing Him—
recognizing Who He is and responding to Him accordingly. Remember,
"Favour is deceitful, and beauty is vain: but a woman that feareth the
LORD, she shall be praised" (Proverbs 31:30). Are you wearing your
pearls?

# LEADER'S GUIDE

# SUGGESTIONS FOR LEADERS

The effectiveness of a group Bible study usually depends on two things: (1) the leader herself; and (2) the ladies' commitment to prepare beforehand and interact during the study. You cannot totally control the second factor, but you have total control over the first one. These brief suggestions will help you be an effective Bible study leader.

You will want to prepare each lesson a week in advance. During the week, read supplemental material and look for illustrations in the everyday events of your life as well as in the lives of others.

Encourage the ladies in the Bible study to complete each lesson before the meeting itself. This preparation will make the discussion more interesting. You can suggest that ladies answer two or three questions a day as part of their daily Bible reading time rather than trying to do the entire lesson at one sitting.

You may also want to encourage the ladies to memorize the key verse for each lesson. (This is the verse that is printed in italics at the start of each lesson.) If possible, print the verses on 3" x 5" cards to distribute each week. If you cannot do this, suggest that the ladies make their own cards and keep them in a prominent place throughout the week.

The physical setting in which you meet will have some bearing on the study itself. An informal circle of chairs, chairs around a table, someone's living room or family room—these types of settings encourage people to relax and participate. In addition to an informal setting, create an atmosphere in which ladies feel free to participate and be themselves.

During the discussion time, here are a few things to observe.

• Don't do all the talking. This study is not designed to be a lecture.

• Encourage discussion on each question by adding ideas and questions.

• Don't discuss controversial issues that will divide the group. (Differences of opinion are healthy; divisions are not.)

• Don't allow one lady to dominate the discussion. Use statements such as these to draw others into the study: "Let's hear from someone on this side of the room" (the side opposite the dominant talker); "Let's hear from someone who has not shared yet today."

• Stay on the subject. The tendency toward tangents is always possible in a discussion. One of your responsibilities as the leader is to keep the group on track.

• Don't get bogged down on a question that interests only one person.

You may want to use the last fifteen minutes of the scheduled time for prayer. If you have a large group of ladies, divide into smaller groups for prayer. You could call this the "Share and Care Time."

If you have a morning Bible study, encourage the ladies to go out for lunch with someone else from time to time. This is a good way to get acquainted with new ladies. Occasionally you could plan a time when ladies bring their own lunches or salads to share and eat together. These things help promote fellowship and friendship in the group.

The formats that follow are suggestions only. You can plan your own format, use one of these, or adapt one of these to your needs.

### 2-hour Bible Study

10:00—10:15   Coffee and fellowship time
10:15—10:30   Get-acquainted time
Have two ladies take five minutes each to tell something about themselves and their families.
Also use this time to make announcements and, if appropriate, take an offering for the baby-sitters.
10:30—11:45   Bible study
Leader guides discussion of the questions in the day's lesson.
11:45—12:00   Prayer time

### 2-hour Bible Study

10:00—10:45   Bible lesson
Leader teaches a lesson on the content of the material. No discussion during this time.
10:45—11:00   Coffee and fellowship
11:00—11:45   Discussion time
Divide into small groups with an appointed leader for each group. Discuss the questions in the day's lesson.
11:45—12:00   Prayer time

### 1½-hour Bible Study

10:00—10:30   Bible study
Leader guides discussion of half the questions in the day's lesson.
10:30—10:45   Coffee and fellowship
10:45—11:15   Bible study
Leader continues discussion of the questions in the day's lesson.
11:15—11:30   Prayer time

# ANSWERS FOR LEADER'S USE

Information inside parentheses ( ) is additional instruction for the group leader.

## LESSON 1

1. David and Bathsheba.

2. Peaceable.

3. (a) Jedidiah. (b) Beloved of the Lord.

4. (a) Be strong; prove yourself a man; keep God's charges; walk in His ways; keep His statutes, commandments, judgments, and testimonies. (b) Solomon would prosper in all he did.

5. He wanted an understanding heart so he could judge the people and discern good and evil.

6. Solomon would have a wise and understanding heart AND riches and honor.

7. Two women had babies. One baby died in the night, and that baby's mother claimed the live baby. When the women took their case to Solomon, he offered to cut the baby in half. The mother of the live baby said no; the other mother said divide him. Thus Solomon knew who was the true mother of the baby.

8. Knowledge—facts and ideas acquired by study, investigation, observation, or experience. Wisdom—marked by deep understanding, keen discernment, and a capacity for sound judgment. Differences—knowledge focuses on "book learning"; wisdom is the right use of one's knowledge.

9. Some smart people are unwise, and some uneducated people are very wise. Smart people can live foolishly. Uneducated people can be wise in the Biblical sense. (Ask someone to read Acts 4:13, a Biblical example of men who were uneducated but wise.)

10. The Lord.

11. (a) The fear of the Lord. (b) Not fear as in afraid, but fear as in awe and reverence; reverential trust. (c) When we have proper reverence for Who God is, we will be able to live in a way that honors Him.

12. It makes one happy; it is more valuable than silver and gold and more precious than rubies; it can increase one's life; its ways are pleasant and peaceful; it gives life.

13. It is better to be wise than rich; better to have understanding than silver.

14. Various answers are possible, including the ideas that he had seen the value of wisdom in everyday life; he knew the results of not acting wisely; he had benefited from acting wisely.

15. Proverbs 3:13—happy; 9:8, 9; 17:10—profits from rebuke and correction; 12:15—heeds counsel; 14:16—fears evil and departs from it; 16:21—is prudent (able to govern and discipline oneself); 3:35—inherits glory or honor.

16. (a) The wisdom of God. (b) Wisdom. (Present the plan of salvation. *Discuss:* Why is the preaching of the gospel considered foolishness by many people? What kinds of things do people try to do to win God's favor?)

*Proverbs in Practice:* Ask the group to share their answers to number 1. In discussing question 2, help the class realize that it does not take a great deal of intelligence to be rightly related to God. Some class members may have some examples to share on this point. Question 3 will help you point out that we can never rest on our laurels. We must keep growing in Christ and keep that relationship vital, or we can easily—and quickly—slide back into our old ways. Questions 4 and 5 are personal answers.

## LESSON 2

1. Awe and reverence; reverential trust.

2. Deuteronomy 33:27—He is eternal; Malachi 3:6—He is immutable, unchanging; 1 Kings 8:27—He is transcendent, infinite; Psalm 99:9—He is holy; Psalm 11:7—He is righteous; Psalm 135:6—He is sovereign; He does what He pleases; Genesis 18:25—He is just; He does what is right; Genesis 17:1—He is almighty, omnipotent (the all-sufficient One); Psalm 139:7-11—He is omnipresent; Acts 15:18—He is omniscient; 1 John 4:7, 8—He is love.

3. (a) We can have confidence and a place of refuge. (b) The more we know Him, the more we trust Him. Confidence and trust go hand in hand.

4. (a) A fountain of life and departure from the snares of death. (b) Physically, we should live a cleaner, healthier life; spiritually, knowing God is the basis for eternal life.

5. (a) Life and true satisfaction. (b) Realizing all God is should lead us to find contentment in Him.

6. (a) Fearing the Lord is the starting point of knowledge. (b) All wisdom and knowledge begin with God. To know Him is the starting place of all other knowledge.

7. Happiness.

8. Keeps us from evil.

9. Proverbs 28:14—falls into mischief; 19:23—visited with evil; 10:27—shortened years; 1:29-32—destroyed by their own devices.

10. He recognized that if he sinned with Potiphar's wife, he was really sinning against God.

11. He recognized the sovereignty of God in all that had happened in his life.

12. (a) He saw a heavenly scene and recognized the holiness of God. (b) He saw himself as sinful and unclean. He was ready to do whatever God desired.

13. "I don't even know Who God is. Why should I obey Him?"

(If you have unsaved class members, take a few minutes to talk about the closing paragraphs of the lesson. Emphasize why God "wrapped Himself in human flesh," and present the plan of salvation.)

*Proverbs in Practice:* Numbers 1 and 2 are personal exercises. Discuss question 3. The basic idea is that a person's lifestyle and speech will honor the Lord. Ask class members to share some ideas on question 4. Possible answers include keeping focused on Who God is; reading the Bible daily (regular exposure to the Word of God is the idea of Deuteronomy 4:10; see Deuteronomy 17:18 and 19 for daily reading of the Word); memorizing verses that exalt the Lord; asking God to help you fear Him (Ps. 86:11).

## LESSON 3

1. He hid his face.

2. He abhorred himself and repented in dust and ashes.

3. He considered himself ignorant and unlearned.

4. He fell at Christ's feet as dead.

5. They cast their crowns before Him and worshiped Him.

6. In order to have skill in godly living—the meaning of wisdom in Proverbs—we need to see ourselves as we really are in relation to Who God really is.

7. 1 Corinthians 4:7—everything we have comes from God; we should not glory as though we had produced it; Isaiah 26:12—everything we accomplish is really God's doing; 1 Corinthians 15:10—Paul accomplished what he did by the grace of God—not by his own strength; Deuteronomy 8:17, 18—the Israelites were to remember that God gave them the ability to get wealth; it was not of their own doing.

8. Let someone else exalt you rather than exalting yourself and then

being put down; let someone else praise you rather than bragging on yourself.

9. (This is a good question for the class members to discuss. Bring out the idea that it is not necessary to be self-abasing; often a sincere "thank you" is sufficient.)

10. The way up is the way down. God will see to it that the humble person receives the honor she is due.

11. (a) Jesus Christ. (b) He left Heaven and came to earth; He was willing to be a servant; He died on the cross. (c) God has highly exalted the Lord Jesus. Someday every knee will bow before Him. (d) Have the same spirit of humility.

12. It is sin.

13. It is abomination to Him; He hates it.

14. Shame.

15. Pride brings destruction.

16. (a) He was filled with pride. (b) He was driven from men and ate grass like an ox; he was deranged. (c) He magnified Who God is and realized God was able to put down the proud.

17. (a) He let the people praise him as a god; he was proud. (b) God punished him immediately. He was eaten by worms and died.

(This lesson provides another opportunity to present the gospel. Talk about what it means to come to Christ in childlike submission and faith.)

*Proverbs in Practice:* Ask the group to share some responses to question 1. Question 2 is personal and should not be discussed in class. You could do some simple role-play situations to answer question 3. Here are some scenarios: one person compliments another on her noticeable weight loss; one person compliments another on a child's accomplishments at school or in sports; one person compliments another on a job promotion. Discuss some possible answers to question 4. Ideas include letting someone with fewer groceries go ahead of you in the line; letting a driver pull out in front of you; giving up something you wanted to do in order to do something someone else wants to do.


## LESSON 4

1. Honesty is a refusal to lie, steal, or deceive in any way. Integrity is trustworthiness and incorruptibility to the extent that one will not be false to a trust, responsibility, or pledge.

2. Marked by strong or strict adherence to moral principles.

3. God hates dishonest dealings; He delights in honest ones. (Have two group members look up Leviticus 19:35 and 36 and Deuteronomy 25:13-16 to find out what the Mosaic law taught about weights.)

4. We need to be honest in all our dealings; e.g., an honest day's work for a day's pay; returning change if we've been given too much; charging people for work actually done.

5. To be poor but be a person of integrity is better than to be rich by crooked means. It is better to be poor and honest than rich and wicked.

6. (a) Jehoiada the priest made a chest with a hole in the lid. When people brought their offerings to the temple, the priests put the money into the chest. (b) No accounting or oversight of the men and money was necessary because the men acted with complete honesty.

7. He hates a lying tongue and a false witness; He delights in lips that deal truly; i.e., those who tell the truth.

8. Perhaps because it is one of Satan's hallmarks; see John 8:44. It was his lie in Genesis 3:4 and 5 that led to Adam and Eve's disobedience and sin. Lying is often at the root of many other sins.

9. Those who defile, cause abomination, or love and practice lies.

10. To put away lying and to speak the truth.

11. Truthful lips will be established forever; lying lips will be punished. Truth endures; lying does not.

12. A false witness will be punished; a liar will not escape.

13. Such gain is a "fleeting fantasy." Wealth acquired in dishonest ways will not last. Seeking money dishonestly is like seeking death.

14. (a) They sold land and brought the money to the apostles. They made it appear they were bringing all the money they gained; in fact, they brought only part of it. (b) Each of them was struck dead by God. (c) God (the Holy Spirit).

15. The upright person is guided by integrity; the perverse person is destroyed by his duplicity.

16. The person of integrity walks securely; she doesn't have to explain herself or make excuses. The perverse person will be found out; she will be discovered for what she truly is.

17. He made Joseph overseer of his house and put everything under Joseph's authority.

18. He fled, leaving his garment behind. He chose not to sin against God.

*Proverbs in Practice:* Question 1 is a personal question, but question 2 will provide a good basis for discussion. In discussing question 3, help the group realize that sometimes it is better to say nothing—even if it is true—than to speak in an unloving way. Close the session with a brief time of silent prayer, using question 4 and Proverbs in Prayer as the basis of the prayer time.

## LESSON 5

1. Lazy—disinclined to activity or exertion. Sluggard—an habitually lazy person.

2. (a) One's heart. (Point out that "kept" means "guarded above all else.") (b) The mind, or inner being; the "real you." (In *Vine's Complete Expository Dictionary,* "heart" is defined as "the inner being of man, the man himself. As such, it is the fountain of all he does.")

3. All we say or think comes from the heart. If we don't keep our hearts diligently, they will lead us astray.

4. She does not love sleep. She gets up and gets going.

5. She becomes poor; she won't have enough food to eat. The person who loves sleep is lazy.

6. Lying around, not having the discipline to get up and get going, is characteristic of a lazy person. And a lazy person does not accomplish much; she does not realize her potential. In addition, a person who cannot discipline herself to get up and get going in the morning will probably have trouble doing her household duties or holding a job.

7. She finds favor and avoids evil. Goodness comes back to her.

8. Proverbs 22:13—I can't go outside; there may be a lion in the street that will kill me; 20:4—It's too cold to plow now. He probably put it off when the weather was good for plowing!

9. He is brother to him who is a great waster. "A poor or unfinished job differs little from a project that someone demolished; both projects are valueless" (Walvoord and Zuck, p. 944).

10. He has plenty. He reaps the rewards of his labor.

11. We need to be diligent in doing whatever is required to provide for our families. (Have volunteers look up and read the New Testament teaching in this regard: 1 Thessalonians 4:11, 12; 2 Thessalonians 3:10, 11; 1 Timothy 5:8.)

12. She shall stand before kings. The idea is that a diligent worker will be promoted. She will not languish in obscurity.

13. Personal answers.

14. Her soul is made fat, meaning "abundantly satisfied." (It's okay to have a fat soul!)

15. Verse 13—she works with her hands; verse 14—she is a good shopper; verse 15—she gets up early in order to work for her family; verse 16—she's a good financial manager; verse 17—she has a good attitude toward work; verse 18—she plans ahead; she doesn't run out of oil for the lamps (the idea of her lamp not going out); verses 19-21—she works to make clothes for her family; they are ready when cold weather comes; verse 27—she is not idle.

16. She fears the Lord.

*Proverbs in Practice:* Discuss question 1. Possible answers include keep reading God's Word; be careful what you watch and listen to and read; stay away from mental junk; engage in wholesome activities. Question 2 should evoke some good responses from the class members. Help them see that a good start is not enough. It takes diligence to keep at a project and have success. Question 3 is personal, but you may want to ask for volunteers to share their answers to question 4.

## LESSON 6

1. Do not eat more than you need. "Excess, even of a good thing, is bad" *(Ryrie Study Bible).*

2. (a) Put a knife to your throat—rather than to your food! (b) Eating with a king. (c) Exercise caution when someone entertains you. His or her hospitality may have a hidden agenda.

3. Do not mix with heavy drinkers or gluttons.

4. Use of alcoholic beverages.

5. (a) The same things he ate and drank. (b) Defiling himself. (c) After ten days of pulse (vegetables) and water, the four Hebrews were healthier and looked better than the young men who ate the king's food.

6. Holds her peace or keeps silent. These verses may have given rise to this advice: It's better to hold your peace and be thought a fool than to open your mouth and dispel all doubt.

7. She is wise.

8. Possible answers include harsh criticism, gossip, complaining.

9. She keeps her soul from trouble.

10. Possible answers include less conflict, less regret over harsh words.

11. It cannot be tamed; it is an unruly evil, full of deadly poison.

12. (Ask someone to quote today's Bible verse [Prov. 16:32] before answering the question.) Better than the mighty and one who can capture a city. "Conquering oneself . . . is of greater virtue than conquering a city" (Walvoord and Zuck, p. 942).

13. A city that is broken down and without walls. It is a position of vulnerability. (*Discuss:* To what problems does a person expose herself if she is quick-tempered?)

14. She exalts folly.

15. Possible answers include becoming alienated from people; living with the guilt and regret of the outcome of a quick temper.

16. To overlook a transgression.

17. Bring into captivity every thought to the obedience of Christ.

18. We are what we think. Eventually we act what we think. Someone has said that we may not be what we think we are, but what we think, we are.

19. A heart that deviseth wicked imaginations, or evil thoughts or schemes.

20. Things that are true, honest, just, pure, lovely, of good report.

*Proverbs in Practice:* Ask the group to share some responses to question 1. Questions 2 and 3 are personal. Answers to question 4 include what we see, read, and hear. Read through the list of questions that make up number 5. Ask the class members to honestly evaluate themselves in this regard. Close in prayer, asking God to help each member practice self-control in the week ahead.

## LESSON 7

1. We become like the people with whom we associate. Choose friends who will lift you up to a higher level, who will challenge and stretch you. Conversely, making unwise choices will eventually cause harm.

2. (a) Iron sharpens iron; the idea of honing a knife. (Demonstrate this if you have a small whetstone and a paring knife.) (b) A friend should bring out the best qualities in the other person. "People can help each other improve by their discussions, criticisms, suggestions, and ideas" (Walvoord and Zuck, p. 964).

3. (a) Friendship with an angry or furious person. (b) You will learn his ways and be ensnared. The idea of a snare is to get trapped in something from which you cannot escape.

4. (a) A talebearer or flatterer; i.e., a person who talks too much. (b) The person may be insincere or even false.

5. (a) Don't mix with drunkards or gluttons. (b) Excessive eating or drinking. (c) Self-control.

6. Evil men; i.e., people who devise violence or plan troublemaking. Don't even desire to be with them. (*Discuss:* How can you help your teenagers see the wisdom of this verse? [One idea is to have them memorize it!] How would practicing the truth of this verse help teens with peer pressure?)

7. Wealthy people have many so-called friends. The relationship usually ends when the money ends.

8. No one was around to help him when the party was over. He found work feeding a farmer's pigs.

9. Keep confidences. To talk too much will separate even close friends. A trustworthy friend keeps her mouth shut.

10. Loves all the time and stands by her friend in hard times.

11. A good friend may offer rebuke or criticism, but she does it for our good. (Ask the ladies if any of them can share an illustration of this verse.)

12. A good friend gives good counsel.

13. The youngest son of Jesse, a shepherd. He was anointed to be king of Israel.

14. The son of Saul, who was the king of Israel.

15. They loved each other deeply—not sexual love, but brotherly love. They were soul mates. Jonathan gave gifts to David as signs of their friendship.

16. They kissed each other and wept; they pledged their undying friendship to each other.

17. They loved deeply; they stood by each other; they kept confidence; Jonathan gave David good counsel.

(Review the plan of salvation if you have unsaved ladies in your Bible study.)

*Proverbs in Practice:* Discuss question 1, especially if some ladies are parents of young children. Ask several volunteers to share their answers to number 2. Questions 3, 4, and 5 are personal. Offer to meet with anyone who has questions about what it means to trust Christ for salvation.

## LESSON 8

1. It is built and established by wisdom and understanding; by knowledge its rooms are filled with pleasant and precious riches. "Folly and sin do

not contribute to security and prosperity, but wisdom does" (Walvoord and Zuck, p. 958).

2. Love and peace.

3. One where the people in it are upright or righteous.

4. He should find all his fulfillment with her; he should be satisfied with her and not be looking to other "cisterns" or "wells." He should be exhilarated with her love.

5. Praised her.

6. Praise indicates value and worth.

7. A good thing.

8. The heart of the husband trusts his wife and he lacks nothing; the wife brings good, not harm, to her husband all the days of her life.

9. She is a crown to her husband.

10. It is better to be in crowded or lonely places than to be in a big house with a brawling, contentious, or angry woman. A miserable woman makes a miserable home!

11. She is quarrelsome. (Share this Arab proverb with the class. You may want to write it on the board. Three things make a house intolerable: tak [the leaking through of rain], nak [a wife's nagging], and bak [bugs].)

12. Train their children.

13. Proverbs 13:24—chasten in love; 23:13—don't withhold correction; 19:18—don't be dissuaded by a child's tears; 22:15—discipline helps dispel folly in a child's attitude; 29:15—an undisciplined child brings shame to his parents; 29:17—a disciplined child is a delight to his parents.

14. Proverbs 2:1, 5—the child will understand the fear of the Lord and find the knowledge of God; 3:1, 2—a disciplined child has a peaceful, long life; 4:20-22—obeying parents brings life; 6:20, 22—obeying parents' commands will lead, keep, and talk (speak) with the child; obedience is a guide, it sets boundaries; 23:24, 25—an obedient child is his parents' delight.

15. Proverbs 15:20—he despises his mother; 17:25—he is a grief to his father and bitterness to his mother; 19:27—he will stray.

16. Husband Elimelech, wife Naomi, and sons Mahlon and Chilion.

17. Orpah and Ruth.

18. Boaz and Ruth are a happily married couple, and they have a baby boy. Naomi is the doting grandmother, who willingly cares for her new little grandson. The whole scene is one of love and contentment.

19. Obed (Ruth's child) was Solomon's great grandfather.

*Proverbs in Practice:* Ask volunteers to share things they do in their homes to have peaceful mealtimes (question 1). Ask members to share some of their paraphrases in response to question 2. Question 3 is personal. Ask ladies to share their answers to questions 4, 5, and 6.

## LESSON 9

(For a different approach in this lesson, divide the class into six groups. Assign the lesson sections as follows to the groups: gossip, lying, flattery, corrupt speech, true words and appropriate words, and helpful words. Allow about five minutes for each group to share answers and prepare to summarize its section. Give each group two to three minutes to present its summary to the rest of the class.)

1. A rumor or report of an intimate nature that reveals personal or sensational information.

2. No. It can be entirely true, but it is information that should not be told.

3. Friendship is ruined because friends are separated.

4. Hearing gossip is like eating something special, a delicacy; not everyone knows it.

5. We should not listen to someone who gossips.

6. A lying tongue; a false witness who speaks lies; he that sows discord among brethren.

7. It was a lie that first caused Eve to listen to Satan. Lying is often at the root of other sins.

8. Lying or falsehood. "Fearing the Lord involves hating what God hates. Since He hates falsehood (12:22), so do the righteous" (Walvood and Zuck, p. 933).

9. A prince or ruler. A civic leader should be a person of his word. (*Ask:* Is this a trait [truthfulness] that we usually associate with politicians today?)

10. Flattery is insincere or excessive praise. Because it is usually insincere, it is not truthful.

11. Ruin.

12. He spreads a net for his feet. A woman who flatters will be caught in her own trap.

13. Constructive criticism (rebuke).

14. Put away a froward, or perverse, mouth; in other words, don't use corrupt words.

15. Possible answers include dirty jokes, swearing, four-letter words.

16. (a) She falls into mischief, or trouble. (b) Possible answers include getting in trouble at home, school, or work because of bad language; offending other people with bad language and perhaps losing friends or acquaintances.

17. They are a sign of righteousness; they endure forever; they bring delight to God.

18. (a) Acceptable, or fitting. (b) Possible answers include sincere praise, encouragement, wise counsel.

19. A soft answer; it turns away wrath. "Being conciliatory in such a [tense] situation requires forethought, patience, self-control, and kindness, virtues commonly lauded in Proverbs" (Walvoord and Zuck, p. 937).

20. Using appropriate words brings joy; a timely word is good.

21. (Ask volunteers to share their answers.)

22. They are sweet to the soul and can even have beneficial physical results.

23. Apples of gold in pictures, or settings, of silver.

24. (a) Cheers a person; makes her glad. (b) (Ask two or three volunteers to give an example.)

25. The words are life-giving; they restore a person rather than tear her down; they are restoring.

26. (a) It promotes health. (b) Answers could include relationships between marriage partners, parents and children, friends, work partners; bringing two factions together.

27. Luke 4:22—gracious words; Matthew 7:29—authoritative words; Mark 10:16—words of blessing; John 8:11—words of forgiveness; John 14:1—words of comfort.

28. It keeps us out of trouble.

29. Not speaking hastily; thinking before we speak.

30. "God, keep a guard, or soldier, at my lips. Help me keep my mouth shut when I should!" (Ask two or three volunteers to read their prayers.)

*Proverbs in Practice:* Discuss some possible answers to question 1. Help the class members realize that sometimes we have to physically remove ourselves from the presence of a person who wants to gossip. Some of the same strategies apply to question 2. Ask for any further suggestions. Possible answers for number 3 include write a note, send a card, write out a Bible promise. Question 4 is a personal answer.

Close the Bible study with the words of Psalm 19:14. Ask God to help each class member with her speech this week.

## LESSON 10

1. By working for it, by diligent labor.

2. Don't get money in sinful or deceitful ways.

3. Possible answers include theft, fraud, lotteries, and gambling.

4. Her greed takes away her life. She will be consumed by her pursuits.

5. She plans, or sets goals.

6. (a) Just what we need. (b) If we have too much, we may become self-sufficient and forget God; if we have too little, we may seek the wrong ways to get what we need.

7. It is better to have a little and fear the Lord than to have a lot of money and a lot of trouble.

8. Don't go into debt. The borrower serves the lender. (*Discuss:* Does this verse mean you should not have a mortgage on your home? A large purchase, such as a house or a vehicle, should be within reason for our incomes, and payments should be part of the monthly budget and made on time.)

9. Righteous people do not squander their money on foolish pursuits. They are more apt to invest in things that have eternal value. They are careful with the money God entrusts to them. They are rich in things money can't buy.

10. (a) Provide an inheritance for your children. (b) No; the Bible teaches us to leave an inheritance.

11. Honor the Lord with the way you use your money.

12. Give to those who need it.

13. (a) We gain by giving. "The hand that gives gathers." You can give, but increase; you can withhold, but become poor. (b) "It is more blessed to give than to receive" is another way of saying that a woman who gives freely gains even more.

14. (a) The Lord. (b) When we give to the poor, hungry, and needy, we are giving to the Lord Himself.

15. Love and peace.

16. Righteousness and integrity.

17. Those gained by lying or violence.

18. Don't get too rich, and don't desire to be poor. Both lead to wrong actions. Be content with what you have.

19. Save during times of plenty so you have something when hard times come.

20. Make good investments.

21. (a) They gave out of deep poverty, but they were actually rich. (b) Gave themselves to the Lord.

22. (a) They gave to Paul's ministry on several occasions. (b) God would supply their need.

*Proverbs in Practice:* Ask if any volunteers want to share their answers to number 1. Questions 2 and 3 are personal answers. Ask question 4 this way: How can the principles in this lesson help you work with a couple who may be having financial problems? Share answers to question 5.